T0161323

BILLEH NICKERSON

IMPACT

THE TITANIC POEMS

BILLEH NICKERSON

IMPACT

THE TITANIC POEMS

ARSENAL PULP PRESS * VANCOUVER

In loving memory of my grandmother,
Hilda Marie Merrimen.

IMPACT: The Titanic Poems
Copyright © 2012 by Billeh Nickerson

ARSENAL PULP PRESS
Suite 101, 211 East Georgia St.
Vancouver, BC
Canada V6A 1Z6
arsenalpulp.com

The publisher gratefully acknowledges the support of the Canada Council for the Arts and the British Columbia Arts Council for its publishing program, and the Government of Canada (through the Canada Book Fund) and the Government of British Columbia (through the Book Publishing Tax Credit Program) for its publishing activities.

Book design by Cynara Geissler
Photograph on frontispiece by Henry W. Clarke, Chief Engineer of Southampton Docks, courtesy of the Vancouver Maritime Museum

Printed and bound in Canada

Library and Archives Canada Cataloguing in Publication:

Nickerson, Billeh, 1972-
        Impact : the Titanic poems / Billeh Nickerson.

Issued also in electronic formats.
ISBN 978-1-55152-442-9

        1. Titanic (Steamship)—Poetry. I. Title.

PS8577.I32I56 2012   C811'.6   C2012-900501-0

I. CONSTRUCTION

II. MAIDEN VOYAGE

III. IMPACT

IV. VOICES

V. IMPACT

VI. DISCOVERY

I. CONSTRUCTION

THE LOST WORKER

Whether the rumours resulted from the faint clangs,
or the faint clangs resulted from the rumours,

even the oldest believed the possibility
of a lost worker could only be an omen.

No matter their sense of wonder,
the pending deadlines, or their hurried pace,

in the back of some workers' minds
their rivets sealed more than just the hull.

At home they hugged their children,
kissed their wives

or dreamed of families
they had yet to realize.

In the back of some workers' minds
their rivets sealed more than just the hull.

HARLAND AND WOLFF

At six-twenty each morning
workers would congregate
by the green gates, often arriving early
to avoid the crush of thousands
for the sooner they reached
their work stations,
the sooner they started
to earn a wage.

Those arriving late
were literally locked out
and would lose a whole day's pay
not to mention the funds spent
holed up at the public house
avoiding home.

THE HATS

Most workers wore duncher caps
save for the foremen
who wore bowlers
and The Hats
who'd enter the main office
in top hats black
as a stoker's coal-covered face.

THE RIVETING SQUAD—
THE HEATER BOYS

They could tell a rivet's temperature
by its colour
and once it reached 650 degrees
it seemed as if they channelled Hephaestus,
the Greek god of fire,
for when they extracted rivets
with their tongs,
it looked like they were throwing
miniature lightning bolts
to the Catch Boys.

THE RIVETING SQUAD—
THE CATCH BOYS

Often as young as thirteen or fourteen,
they'd catch the rivet
in a tin, grab the scorching metal
with their tongs
and then, as if passing a baton
in a relay, run full-tilt
to the Holder-Ons.

THE RIVETING SQUAD—
THE HOLDER-ONS

They'd help place the rivet
in the desired hole
and secure it with little more
than determination
and a fourteen-pound hammer
for the Riveters.

THE RIVETING SQUAD—
THE RIVETERS

They needed to wear scarves
around their necks
all year long, no matter the weather,
to stop bits of rivet ember
from getting down their shirts,
burning through their skin.
They'd stand on opposite sides,
clang – clang clang – clang clang – clang
to shape everything into place.

GOOSE BUMPS

It took three million rivets
to piece the ship together

though only a few seconds
for a small child to notice

it was as if the ship
had a surprise chill

for it seemed her hull
was covered in goose bumps.

A GIANT ELM TREE

Perhaps it was simply
the colour

of her copper propellers
that drew comparisons

to giant elm trees,
a tip of the hat

to the earthy hue
amongst all that grey.

Or perhaps it was a desire
to connect with nature

in some way,
an organic cousin

when the politics
of scale veered

so far into the realm
of manmade.

Twenty-two tons of train oil, tallow and soap,
and a father as he explains to his son
the art of friction—
it's like when your hand got stuck
in grandma's vase and your mother rubbed
butter around your wrist,
how you slid free
as easily as the *Titanic* slid in.

THE CLOTHESLINE

One woman grew accustomed
to seeing the great ship
whenever she unpinned her laundry.

Sometimes it was an apron
or one of her husband's shirts,
clothing large enough

that when removed
it framed a portrait
of the *Titanic* in the distance.

On laundry day after the launch,
she kept squinting
in hopes her eyes had failed her,

the familiar view now missing,
as if a sleeping giant woke up
and walked away.

II. MAIDEN VOYAGE

JENNY THE CAT

Jenny delivered her kittens
in the weeks that preceded the maiden voyage.

As if she could sense the impending disaster,
she carried her kittens by the neck,

one by one, down the gangplank
to the quay at Southampton

and in those moments convinced
one of the stokers to accept employment

somewhere else, for even though
his impending two-week contract paid well,

he learned long ago to always trust
a mother's instincts.

HER PASSENGERS

American,
Australian,
Austro-Hungarian,
Belgian,
British,
Bulgarian,
Canadian,
Chinese,
Danish,
Dutch,
Finnish,
French,
German,
Greek,
Italian,
Irish,
Japanese,
Mexican,
Norwegian,

Portugese,
Russian,
South African,
Spanish,
Swedish,
Swiss,
Syrian,
Turkish,
Uruguayan.

SELECTED PROVISIONS

Fruits

36,000 oranges
36,000 apples
16,000 lemons
13,000 grapefruits
1,000 lbs grapes

Vegetables

40 tons potatoes
7,000 heads of lettuce
3,500 onions
2,250 lbs fresh green peas
800 bundles asparagus

Meats

75,000 lbs beef
25,000 lbs poultry and game

11,000 lbs fresh fish
7,500 lbs bacon and ham
2,500 lbs sausages

Baking

40,000 eggs
10,000 lbs sugar
6,000 lbs butter
1,500 g fresh milk
250 barrels flour

Tobacco

8,000 cigars

CAPTAIN SMITH'S BEARD

For many passengers,
his well-groomed appearance
solidified their trust,

as if his shaving precision
somehow reflected
his seamanship.

Young crewmen coveted his beard
as if it were an achievement
like the four stripes
that adorned his sleeves
and epaulettes.

They dreamed of the day
their follicles could be let loose,
a well-maintained field
in a life so full of ocean.

Sometimes he'd recognize himself
as a proud husband and father,
a veteran of the Boer War,
The White Star Line's esteemed
and decorated Captain,

while other times it seemed
the young boy who left
for a career at sea
stared back from behind
his white mask.

THE SWIMMING POOL

Though most would not need to,
some high-society ladies practiced
their strokes each morning
while servants stood poolside
with long white towels, thick
bathrobes with monogrammed pockets.

One third-class passenger figured
the twenty-five cents admission
an investment, a story he could tell for drinks—
the one about how he swam aboard the *Titanic*,
dove six feet under to the bottom,
and stared up at the world's richest women
as their coloured bathing caps
kept their hair dry and smiles intact.

THE FOURTH SMOKESTACK

Most admirers had no clue
its epic verticality had little purpose
other than aesthetic.
In postcards and posters,
artists depicted huge plumes,
though the only smoke
came from First Class
in the smoking room
for which it served as ventilation.

THE DISTANCE POOL

As if the ship were a newborn
bet on by loved ones
trying to guess her weight,

passengers placed bets
on distance travelled,
and at noon each day

they'd congregate,
wait for the purser
to announce

just how far they had gone
and who among them
won the jackpot.

Harry Anderson's fifty-dollar Chow

Robert W Daniel's champion French Bulldog,
  Gamon de Pycombe

John Jacob Astor's Airedale, *Kitty*

Helen Bishop's *Frou Frou*

Miss Margaret Hays' Pomeranian

Elizabeth Rothschild's Pomeranian

William Ernest Carter's King Charles Spaniel

Henry Sleeper Harper's Pekingese, *Sun Yat Sen*

A YOUNG BOY'S SPINNING TOP

In this picture, a young boy stands transfixed
at the magic of a spinning top.

It doesn't matter that he walks
on the deck of the world's largest ship

or that it's a maiden voyage
and everything is imbued with celebration,

for he's full of wonder and intrigued
at the constant spinning and spinning

as if his joy could be never-ending,
the ship's fate undetermined.

III. IMPACT

IMPACT

One passenger believed it was her husband,
the ship's jolt just another expression of their love.
Others thought it was an earthquake
or a mishap in the galley—
a runaway trolley, a stack of fallen dishes.
The baker wasn't sure what happened
though he hoped his loaves would not fall.

While airtight after airtight compartment filled,
a second-class passenger ordered his drink
with chunks from the berg.
A small child sucked pieces of ice
as if they were candies,
and her brothers scraped up snowballs,
their mother worried only
they could lose an eye.

THE PROGNOSIS

After Thomas Andrews returned to the bridge
from examining the damage below,

he realized how a doctor must feel
when delivering a negative prognosis.

While Captain Smith expected the ailment
to only be minor, a strain or sprain,

Andrews worked hard for the words
to explain their condition,

how they should all find ways
to get their personal affairs in order.

THE BARBER

Up until now, his only worries were
rough seas and dull scissors,
but with each launched lifeboat he gained
perspective and a newfound clarity—
the piles of hair, the polite conversations
where he'd nod yes even when he meant no,
a life's worth of postcard sales, miniature lifesavers,
and the pennants that hung from the ceiling.
He considered how early barbers worked
as dentists and bloodletters—
the spinning pole outside his shop
symbolizing blue blood to the heart,
red blood to the body.
Most customers thought it was a giant candy
like the peppermints
he gave to young boys on their first cut.
He wondered whether he should apologize
for all the missing hairs
for he knew the men would need them,
every last one.

THE BOY IN LIFEBOAT NO. 14

Although the boy had yet to hear
his own voice change or find himself
needing to shave a scruffy face,
Second Officer Lightoller still threatened
to blow the boy's brains out
unless he left the lifeboat
and returned to the sinking ship.
The women pleaded he was only a boy,
that there was room enough
for all of them, but as the lifeboat rocked
like a giant cradle in the wind,
Lightoller maintained a strict adherence
to *women and children first*.
One little girl wondered if jumping
from boat to boat was a game
only boys could play and, if so,
why did he seem upset?
As the older men stood back
with cigars, enjoyed the last

few swigs from favourite flasks,
the boy sat inside a coil of rope,
heavy with the feeling
he'd become a man.

THE WISHING WELL

As her lifeboat lowered,
one woman recalled
a childhood game
where she squeezed
both feet
into the bucket
from a wishing well,
and held on tight
as her brothers
lowered her
down
to the bottom.
She never opened
her eyes,
could only tell
she made it
by the splash
and the lapping sounds
that reminded her

of hunting dogs drinking
from a birdbath
or pond.
As her brothers
pulled her
back up
she'd think
of new excuses
to tell her mother,
yet another puddle,
a spilled glass
of water,
a leaky vase
full of flowers.

EDITH EVANS

A fortune teller once told Edith Evans,
beware of the water. For years she walked
with her head down, convinced that if she didn't
she'd someday step into a puddle,
ruin a new pair of shoes.

When the last lifeboat left without her,
the deck all of a sudden filled with men,
she reached down to her ankles, undid the laces,
threw her shoes into the darkness—and waited,
waited for the splash.

THE PIANO PLAYER

Unlike his musician compatriots
whose instruments could be carried on deck

the ship's piano player could only watch
as his band mates played on.

At first he just swayed to the music
then tapped his feet and hummed

but he couldn't withstand
the ache to play along

even without a sound
his hands slipping from gloves,

his cold fingers
tickling the air, ghost-style.

EPIPHANY

All those years, he'd never harmed her,
not once, until she refused to leave him
and he dragged her by the arm
through the crowd to the lifeboat.
She remembers craning her neck to see past
the hats of the women around her,
how the last time she saw him
the haze of lace atop another woman's head
made it seem like a giant spider's web
had caught him and the ship.
In the weeks that followed, she kept massaging
her arm, watching the bruise change colour.
It wasn't until it faded away
that she believed everything:
the ship sank after the iceberg hit,
her husband never would again.

STEWARD JOHNSTON

As if he worried the women in lifeboat No. 2
would succumb to scurvy,
Steward Johnston filled his pockets with oranges
and later watched as an assembly line
of cold hands passed the small orbs around.
One woman thought it strange to be eating
oranges in the dark and struggled
to peel the skin with her numb fingers,
her taste buds unable to decipher
any sweetness beneath the salt.

SOMEONE'S LUCKY PENNY

slipped out
of his pocket
and drifted
down
for two
hours

IV. VOICES

SECOND OFFICER CHARLES LIGHTOLLER

What I remember that night—
what I will remember as long as I live—
is the people crying out to each other
as the stern began to plunge down.

I heard people crying
I love you.

STEWARDESS VIOLET JESSOP

A few cries came to us across the water,
then silence, as the ship seemed to right herself
like a hurt animal with a broken back.

She settled for a few minutes,
but one more deck of lighted ports
disappeared.

Then she went down
by the head with a thundering roar
of underwater explosions,

our proud ship,
our beautiful *Titanic*
gone to her doom.

It was a noise no one had heard before
and no one wishes to hear again.

It was stupefying, stupendous
as it came to us along the water.

It was if all the heavy things
one could think of

had been thrown downstairs
from the top of a house,

smashing each other, and the stairs
and everything in the way.

EVA HART

When we were in the boat rowing away,
then we could hear the panic,
of people rushing about on the deck
and screaming and looking for lifeboats.
Oh it was dreadful!

The bow went down first and the stern stuck up
in the ocean for what seemed to me a long time,
of course it wasn't, but it stood out stark
against the sky and then heeled over and went down.
You could hear the people screaming and thrashing about.

I remember saying to my mother once
how dreadful that noise was
and I always remember her reply, she said
yes, but think back about the silence that followed,
because all of a sudden it wasn't there—
the ship wasn't there, the lights weren't there
and the cries weren't there.

COLONEL ARCHIBALD GRACIE IV

There arose to the sky
the most horrible sounds
ever heard by mortal man
except by those of us
who survived this terrible tragedy.

The agonizing cries of death
from over a thousand throats,
the wails and groans
of suffering,
none of us will ever forget
to our dying day.

V. IMPACT

CARPATHIA

By chance the *Carpathia*'s wireless operator
kept his headphones on
while undressing before bed

and in what should have been the last moments
of his long shift, he overheard messages
destined for the great ship.

Come at once.
We have struck an ice berg.
It's C.Q.D., Old Man.

When her Captain learned of the disaster,
he ordered heating and hot water turned off
to conserve as much steam as possible,

so that her passengers,
scheduled for sunny Gibraltar,
awoke to cold cabins.

Although designed for only 14.5 knots,
she conjured up 17.5 that night
as she rushed to the rescue.

As she grew closer to the scene,
the Captain ordered rockets fired
every fifteen minutes

as a navigational tool for any lifeboats,
but mostly as inspiration
for those who'd spent all night in the dark.

When she arrived at four a.m.,
her crew couldn't believe
all that remained of the world's largest ship

lay before them in the wreckage
floating amongst the ice
and the lifeboats that speckled the sea.

Surely, there must be something else,
they thought, how could she
just disappear?

FIRST MEMORIAL

Even the children knew not to play
around the mountain of lifejackets
piled on the *Carpathia*'s deck.
How strange they seemed empty,
lifeless on top of lifeless,
their collars looking more and more
like holes.

ROSA ABBOTT

While Rosa Abbott contemplated
how her family might still be together
had her arms only been stronger—
her sons once again pulled from her body,
into the Atlantic cold and un-amniotic—
a fellow passenger combed Rosa's hair,
stroke after stroke, determined to untangle
the piece of cork that lodged itself
while she'd struggled to stay afloat.
It took a long time and with each stroke,
again and again, the repetition lulled them
like the soft strophe of a child's song.

THE YOUNG WIDOW

Of all the widows, newlywed Mary Marvin
had the unfortunate distinction

of being able to watch
her wedding after the fact,

for her husband's father owned
a motion picture company

and made theirs the first wedding
filmed for all to see.

Although she would see her eighteen-year-old self
grow older over the years,

her nineteen-year-old groom was forever
on a film loop, never to change.

THE CARVER

His wife remarked he'd developed
   a carver's tick where he gently blew
on everything he cared for
   as if fine sawdust impeded his view—
be it of her bedtime body or his daughter's forehead.

As a child he whittled away at sticks,
   non-stop it seemed, so that his mother teased
whenever she needed to find him
   she just followed the trail
of his fresh wood shavings.

His father nicknamed him the termite
   and his sisters chastised
for all the wooden bits
   they found
in their petticoats and frilly dresses.

When he grew up a master carver,
   it seemed a perfect fit,

like the way Cinderella's elegant foot
    found a matching slipper,
only this time made of wood.

During his years at Harland and Wolff
    he dreamed in the curlicues
and elaborate patterns handcrafted
    into the oak panels and staircases
that made First Class first class.

The day he learned of the sinking
    he felt an ache not only in his heart,
but in his fingers and in his lips
    as he blew away at the non-existent
sawdust, and cried.

Out in the harbour, one reporter chartered a boat
to shadow the rescue ship,
used a megaphone to tempt the crew

with the promise of a few month's pay
to give an exclusive interview
by jumping overboard and swimming to him.

Thirty thousand gathered that night around the pier,
more than a full house
at major league baseball's Hilltop Park.

Some showed up to confirm
the fate of their loved ones,
others just hoped to satisfy their curiosity

catch a glimpse of the survivors,
the famous, the infamous,
all that spectacle and pain.

GROUP PHOTOGRAPH, SOUTHAMPTON

Someone thought it a good idea to document
the devastation further—as if numbers weren't
vivid enough—the photographer moving them,
boys in back, girls out front,
each of them a relative
of a lost *Titanic* crewman.

It's the same sort of photograph taken
after coal mine disasters or when an entire fleet
from a fishing village goes missing—
in every photograph there's always
an older sister holding a younger sibling
or boys almost old enough for a father to teach them
how to shave. In every photograph there's always
a young girl with a big smile,
just an ordinary girl
smiling.

THE CABLE-SHIP MACKAY-BENNETT

Although it seemed a cruel irony,
the crew stocked her hold
with one-hundred tons of ice.

They covered her decks
with burlap and coffins,
enough embalming fluid for hundreds.

They brought along an Anglican priest,
undertakers who wondered
how they'd work at sea.

Not even double wages
or extra rum rations,
not even reminders

of how much comfort
they'd bring grieving families
could lessen their dread

of the moment
they discovered wreckage
and needed to begin their task.

They had fished all their lives
for haddock, mackerel, and cod,
but never for corpse,

so when they arrived on scene
they thought the white specks
in the distance were seagulls,

not whitecaps caused
by waves breaking
over bodies.

Men in teams of five
lowered themselves into cutters
no larger than *Titanic*'s lifeboats

and in the open ocean
they searched
for those held up by lifejackets,

many with arms outstretched
like sleep walkers,
though they'd never wake again.

Row, situate, grab, and hoist.
Row, situate, grab, and hoist.
Row, situate, grab, and hoist.

They retrieved over 300,
including a young boy,
no more than two years old.

In Halifax, one newspaper
nicknamed her The Death Ship,
as if she were the root

of the tragedy,
and not just another messenger
forever changed

by the knowledge
she brought back
to shore.

TEN MINUTES FAST

He always prided himself on being timely,
set his pocket watch ten minutes fast,
a trait the men in his family shared
along with broad shoulders, dimpled chins,
and a taste for adventure.
Had he travelled with his father or brothers
the embalmer who found him
might not have been surprised
to see the pocket watch indicate two-thirty—
ten minutes after the *Titanic* went down—
but as he travelled alone,
his was the only watch out of step.
At first the embalmer pondered how
he'd cheated the ocean of those precious minutes—
whether he'd stayed afloat
atop a piece of wreckage or treaded water
with the watch held over his head—
then, in an indignity specific to his family,
the embalmer declared he'd arrived late.

THE EMBALMER'S DAUGHTER

Her mother once explained
it was like playing dollies,

dressing people up in their Sunday best,
pretty as a picture, her father's hard work

helping everyone remember
how much they loved someone.

She thought of this whenever
children threw spitballs or rocks,

pulled the ribbons from her hair,
or teased that she smelled like a corpse.

No matter how fragrant the soaps
or expensive the perfumes,

it was if they could smell
the disinfectant and formaldehyde

that followed her family
as fish smell follows fishermen.

When word spread that the boat
filled with the *Titanic* dead

would soon return to Halifax,
she thought of her taunting classmates

and her father's hands working hard
to make things beautiful again.

SAFEKEEPING

Even though they'd both watched rats
scurry across the deck,

Edward Lockyer somehow convinced
Emily Badman that he'd be okay,

that she should enter a lifeboat,
for he would see her later

and could even take her eyeglasses
for safekeeping.

Months later, when opening a parcel,
Emily felt as if she'd seen a ghost

for when Edward's mother received
the personal effects found on her son's body,

she unwittingly kept his promise
and mailed off Emily's eyeglasses,

intact though questionably
no worse for wear.

THOMSON BEATTIE

Though his family understood
the ocean's give and take
as well as anyone,

it was hard for them
not to sense
divine retribution

for when a passing ship discovered
Thomson Beattie's body
one month after the sinking,

it happened near the spot
eighty-two years to the day
where his grandmother

gave birth to his mother
as she crossed the Atlantic
in search of a better life.

THE BALANCE

Although the band played on,
their paycheques stopped
the second the water swept
over the bow.

One family received an invoice
for the balance owing
on their loved one's uniform,
which startled them
as they believed
they'd already paid so much.

THE ROLLING PIN

Salvaged from a block of wood,
a banister perhaps, or something from First Class
found floating amongst the bodies,
Third-Engineer J.A. O'Brien sanded it
smooth as a newborn baby
so sometimes his wife would cradle
or press it to her face.

Although no one would dare mention it,
while watching her from behind
it seemed as if she were rowing,
her arms muscling over the dough,
her pie crusts heavenly,
light as air.

THE SOUND OF DROWNING

Most survivors will tell you
it can't be explained,

the horror when the lights went out,
when nothing was left but voices.

One survivor spent a lifetime trying to forget
everything he'd heard that night—

he moved to the Midwest, replaced the ocean
with plains, a neighbouring baseball field,

but each time the home team cracked one out of the park
he'd think of the lifeboats, the iceberg,

the screams.

J. BRUCE ISMAY

Had he not cancelled the planned extra lifeboats
in favour of additional deck space
and a less encumbered view,

had he heeded the ice warnings
and not pushed the Captain
for a speedy maiden voyage,

had he not taken a seat
when offered
especially with so many stuck below,

had he not holed himself up
in a private cabin
on the rescue ship

while other survivors
crowded together
forced to grieve in public,

perhaps history
would not have been
so unkind,

and the whispers
that followed him
ubiquitous.

VI. DISCOVERY

THE DEBRIS FIELD

In some areas it seems perfect for a picnic—
a sandy blanket, dozens of unbroken plates,
cutlery sparkling like it was buffed
with a napkin or long skirt.
Down here the water is so cold and heavy
time stands still—
even the cheese wheels are edible
and the wine is still as fine
as it was that final night.

EIGHT INCHES APART

Researchers soon determined that micro-organisms disliked
the tannic acid that finished brown leather,

so while they ate away at buttons, satchels, and shoes
from darker goods, they ignored the browns

as if they were stubborn children
determined to reject their vegetables.

While his colleagues marvelled at the realization
of brown leather everything

one researcher wondered why all the shoes
appeared in pairs, and always eight inches apart.

Later, they realized organisms had erased
every sign of existence—the flesh, hair, bone and clothes—

save for a few pieces of jewellery and a pair of shoes
resting the natural distance

between the feet of a prone human body—
eight inches apart, four miles below the surface.

At first it seems like any other cemetery,
a well-kept lawn, granite tombstones,
an unpaved driveway and the crunch of gravel
as the car slows down before a sign:
T I T A N I C
as if the ship were buried here too,
a Viking funeral.

This is where the City of Halifax laid to rest
many of the bodies unclaimed
from the impromptu morgue
at the Mayflower Curling Club,
where tourists take photographs
for vacation albums and young girls
leave panties and love notes
for the crewman with a name similar
to the character played by DiCaprio.

Some graves have only numbers,
the Atlantic pickpocketed the wallet
or purse that would have identified them.

Most are from second and third class,
their families unable to afford
the boat or train trip home.

A hundred years later,
people still bring wreaths, flowers
that survive through snowstorms,
year after year,
spring's first green accompanied
by plastic pink and frosted yellow.

THE LAST SURVIVOR

One-hundred years later,
the final *Titanic* child now buried,

how strange that the last survivor
is the *Titanic* herself.

Some day even she will dissolve
into a golden treacle of rust

until all that remains
is her memory,

a story to hand down
through generations.

NOTE ON THE TEXT

My thanks to the authors, directors, and historians whose works inspired this book. In particular, I'd like to mention Walter Lord, the author of the seminal *Titanic* text, *A Night to Remember,* for his book started my lifelong interest in the ship and her many stories.

Thanks also to the Maritime Museum of the Atlantic in Halifax, Nova Scotia, for its respectful displays, including the rolling pin that inspired my poem of the same name; and to the City of Belfast and its numerous historical sites and museums. It's true she was alright when she left there.

The poems from the section entitled "Voices" are found poems derived from quotes or the writings from the survivors whose names are used in the titles. The Violet Jessop poem is comprised of lines taken from *Titanic Survivor: The Newly Discovered Memoirs of Violet Jessop Who Survived Both the Titanic and the Britannic Disasters.*

THANK YOUS

Thank you to the following journals for publishing many of these poems, sometimes in early versions: *Antigonish Review, Contemporary Verse 2, The Fiddlehead, Grain,* and *PRISM international.*

Thanks also to Lorna Crozier and George McWhirter, whose passion and support were invaluable during my studies with them.

Thanks also to the BC Arts Council Scholarship program for its assistance; to the Writers' Trust of Canada and the Canada Council for the Arts for their support of the Berton House writers' residency in Dawson City, Yukon, where I had the pleasure to work on this collection; and to Kwantlen Polytechnic University for travel funds that allowed me to visit Belfast and Southampton.

This book could not have been written without the editorial (h)ear(t) and the friendship of Sheri-D Wilson.

Thanks to Craig Moseley, Michael V. Smith, Ivan E. Coyote, Elizabeth Bachinsky, Daniel Zomparelli, and the late Matt Davy. I am blessed to have met you all.

Thank you to the fine folks at Arsenal Pulp Press.

BORN IN HALIFAX and raised in Langley, BC, Billeh Nickerson is the author of the poetry collections *The Asthmatic Glassblower* and *McPoems*. He also authored the humour collection *Let Me Kiss It Better,* and is co-editor of *Seminal: The Anthology of Canada's Gay Male Poets.* He performs frequently at literary festivals across Canada and teaches creative writing at Kwantlen Polytechnic University in Vancouver.